FOCUS ON
FAMILY
MATTERS
· · · · · · · · ·

Teen Pregnancy

FOCUS ON FAMILY MATTERS

The Blending of Foster and Adopted Children into the Family

Dealing with Terminal Illness in the Family

Dealing with the Effects of Rape and Incest

The Effects of Job Loss on the Family

Teen Pregnancy

Understanding and Coping with Divorce

Focus on Family Matters

Teen Pregnancy

Michele Alpern

Marvin Rosen, Ph.D.
Consulting Editor

Chelsea House Publishers
Philadelphia

CHELSEA HOUSE PUBLISHERS
EDITOR IN CHIEF Sally Cheney
DIRECTOR OF PRODUCTION Kim Shinners
CREATIVE MANAGER Takeshi Takahashi
MANUFACTURING MANAGER Diann Grasse

Staff for TEEN PREGNANCY
ASSOCIATE EDITOR Bill Conn
PICTURE RESEARCHER Sarah Bloom
PRODUCTION ASSISTANT Jaimie Winkler
SERIES DESIGNER Takeshi Takahashi
LAYOUT 21st Century Publishing and Communications, Inc.

http://www.chelseahouse.com

First Printing

1 3 5 7 9 8 6 4 2

Library of Congress Cataloging-in-Publication Data

Alpern, Michele.
    Teen pregnancy / by Michele Alpern.
        v. cm. — (Focus on family matters)
Includes bibliographical references and index.
Contents: Sexuality and birth control—What if you think you're pregnant—Abortion—Adoption—Being pregnant—Raising a child.
    ISBN 0-7910-6695-9
    1. Teenage pregnancy—Juvenile literature. 2. Teenage mothers—Juvenile literature.
[1. Pregnancy. 2. Teenage mothers.] I. Title. II. Series.
HQ759.4 .A465 2002
306.874'3—dc21

                                                                                        2001008111

Contents

Introduction 6

1 Sexuality and Birth Control 8

2 Dealing with an Unplanned
Pregnancy 18

3 Being Pregnant 26

4 Raising a Child 34

5 Adoption 44

6 Abortion 52

Glossary 60

Further Reading 61

Index 62

Introduction
Marvin Rosen, Ph.D.
Consulting Editor

Bad things sometimes happen to good people. We've probably all heard that expression. But what happens when the "good people" are teenagers?

Growing up is stressful and difficult to negotiate. Teenagers are struggling to becoming independent, trying to cut ties with their families that they see as restrictive, burdensome, and unfair. Rather than attempting to connect in new ways with their parents, they may withdraw. When bad things do happen, this separation may make the teen feel alone in coping with difficult and stressful issues.

Focus on Family Matters provides teens with practical information about how to cope when bad things happen to them. The series deals foremost with feelings—the emotional pain associated with adversity. Grieving, fear, anger, stress, guilt, and sadness are addressed head on. Teens will gain valuable insight and advice about dealing with their feelings, and for seeking help when they cannot help themselves.

The authors in this series identify some of the more serious problems teens face. In so doing, they make three assumptions: First, teens who find themselves in difficult situations are not at fault and should not blame themselves. Second, teens can overcome difficult situations, but may need help to do so. Third, teens bond with their families, and the strength of this bond influences their ability to handle difficult situations.

These books are also about communication—specifically about the value of communication. None of the problems covered occurs in a vacuum, and none of the situations should be faced by anyone alone. Each either involves a close family member or affects the entire family. Since families teach teens how to trust, relate to others, and solve problems, teens need to bond with families to develop normally and become emotionally whole. Success in dealing with adversity depends not only on the strength of the individual teen, but also upon the resources of the family in providing support, advice, and material assistance. Strong attachment to care givers in a supporting, nurturing, safe family structure is essential to successful coping.

Some teens learn to cope with adversity—they absorb the pain, they adjust, and they go on. But for others, the trauma they experience seems like an insurmountable challenge—they become angry, stressed, and depressed. They may withdraw from friends, they may stop going to school, and their grades may slip. They may draw negative attention to themselves and express their pain and fear by rebelling. Yet, in each case, healing can occur.

The teens who cope well with adversity, who are able to put the past behind them and regain their momentum, are no less sensitive or caring than those who suffer most. Yet there is a difference. Teens who are more resilient to trauma are able to dig deep down into their own resources, to find strength in their families and in their own skills, accomplishments, goals, aspirations, and values. They are able to find reasons for optimism and to feel confidence in their capabilities. This series recognizes the effectiveness of these strategies, and presents problem-solving skills that every teen can use.

Focus on Family Matters is positive, optimistic, and supportive. It gives teens hope and reinforces the power of their own efforts to handle adversity. And most importantly, it shows teens that while they cannot undo the bad things that have happen, they have the power to shape their own futures and flourish as healthy, productive adults.

Sexuality and Birth Control

■ Lauren is in love with her boyfriend, and they have sex sometimes. Her boyfriend doesn't use condoms, and she is too shy to ask him to use one. It's such an embarrassing thing to talk about, she doesn't know what she would say to him even if she wanted to.

Lauren doesn't want to go to the doctor for birth control either. The doctor costs money, and what if her parents find out about it? She thinks her mom and dad wouldn't approve, and worse, they would probably want to talk to her boyfriend about it, too. Lauren thinks that things will probably be alright—she's had sex a few times already, and nothing bad has happened.

Every day, teenage women from every background face the challenge of discovering they are pregnant. One million teenage women become pregnant each year in the United States. By age eighteen, one in every four American women gets pregnant. The great majority of teen pregnancies are unplanned, that is, the women didn't mean to get pregnant.

It is important for teenagers to understand why so many young people get pregnant and how to prevent pregnancy. Teenagers also need to understand their options if they do get pregnant. Pregnant women can choose either to raise the child, to place the baby for adoption, or to have an abortion. The decision of how to proceed with a pregnancy is serious. The woman must decide whether to bring a new human being into the world or not. She must decide if she is able and willing to care for a child. The course of action she chooses will affect her health, her finances, and her deepest emotions.

Pregnancy is challenging for both the young woman and young man involved in creating it. Teenagers have fewer resources and less experience than adults. Getting accurate information about pregnancy enables you to make the choices that are best for you. This book provides

> **Where do you find information on dealing with an unplanned pregnancy?**

information about preventing pregnancy and about your options if you do become pregnant. To learn more, you can look into the additional resources listed at the end of this book. In order to make the decisions you are most comfortable with, it is also important that you talk with people you trust—your teacher or school counselor, doctor or health clinician, parents or other relatives—whoever you can count on to give you the help and guidance you need.

Pregnancy is very likely to occur if a woman and a man have **sexual intercourse** without using **birth control**. The first step in understanding teen pregnancy is understanding sexual reproduction and birth control. Many teens do not know the facts about the physical mechanics of sexuality and **contraception** (another word for birth control). Moreover,

Using contraception, like these birth control pills, drastically reduces the risk of getting pregnant. Some teens think obtaining contraceptive devices is too difficult, embarrassing, or expensive; the alternative, however, is dealing with an unplanned pregnancy.

the subject raises a host of factors—biology, desire, cultural and family values, peer pressure—that can be tough for teens to sort out on their own.

Getting pregnant: biology

From adolescence to midlife, the ovaries in a woman's body release eggs. During sexual intercourse, the man's penis releases fluid containing many sperm into the woman's vagina. When birth control is not used, the sperm swim up into the woman's reproductive organs, where they can meet an egg. If a sperm meets an egg, the woman becomes pregnant.

Human biology makes it very probable that sexual intercourse will lead to pregnancy, unless contraception is used. In fact, *four out of every five* teenage women who have intercourse without birth control get pregnant within their first year of sexual activity. If you don't want to become pregnant, you need to consider very carefully whether or not to have sexual intercourse. If you do choose to have intercourse, you must use contraception to reduce the risk of getting pregnant.

Issues for teenagers

In recent years, many teens are choosing to practice **abstinence**, which means that they refrain from sexual activity. The decision to practice abstinence may be grounded in moral or religious beliefs, but it has some very practical health benefits for teens as well. It guarantees that you will not become pregnant unintentionally, and ensures that you will not contract a **sexually transmitted disease** like HIV, gonorrhea, or herpes.

The nature of human sexuality is such that sexual intercourse is closely linked to our emotional and psychological health. Many teens feel that they are not ready to handle the emotions involved a sexual relationship, or the responsibilities that accompany it. So, they choose abstinence, and wait to have

Why would a teenager decide to practice abstinence?

sex until they are in a committed relationship like marriage. Ultimately, the decision to have sex is yours, and you should weigh all of your options as well as the potential consequences, like pregnancy and disease, of your actions.

If you do have sexual intercourse, there is one simple fact that you should keep in mind: birth control must be used during intercourse to prevent pregnancy. What stops these teenagers from using contraception?

Some teen women want to get pregnant. They may feel they are ready to have a baby. Many of these young women are not aware of the huge responsibility that parenthood will bring or how difficult it will be, as a teenager, to manage childrearing.

However, studies show that the vast majority of pregnant teens did not intend or wish to get pregnant. There are a number of hurdles that may keep a teen from using contraception. First, accurate information about birth control may take some effort to find, especially if it is not provided in schools. Teens need to obtain medical information through books or by asking health professionals or other trusted adults. In the absence of facts, false information circulates among teenagers; for example the claim that you can't get pregnant the first time you have sex is completely untrue. Similarly, popular culture—movies, TV, songs—often inaccurately portrays sexual activity; it shows fantasies of casual sex without birth control and does not acknowledge that in real life this would likely lead to pregnancy.

Can you get pregnant the first time you have sex, or if you have sex only once without birth control?

In addition to acquiring factual information, getting contraceptive devices also takes some effort. Birth control costs money, although low-cost contraception is available, as the close of this chapter will discuss. Even more significantly, birth control requires planning. Teenagers often don't think ahead of time that they will have sex; then, when a sexual encounter arises, they haven't thought to have birth control on hand. If you imagine there is any possibility that you may have intercourse in the near future, you need to prepare yourself by obtaining contraception. If you don't have birth control, you must postpone having sex until you have it, or else run the high risk of pregnancy.

Desire is powerful, and in the heat of a sexual encounter, it can be hard to think reasonably. If you don't have contraception, you may be tempted to have sex anyway. Alcohol and drugs cloud your reasoning even more. Almost one half of all unintended teen pregnancies occur when teenagers have sex while under the influence of alcohol or drugs. If you don't want to get pregnant, you must be alert to the way drugs and alcohol cloud your judgment.

Cultural messages that tell teens it is wrong for young people to have sex may also present a challenge for sexually active teenagers. Teenagers who have intercourse may feel that they are doing something wrong or shameful. These teens may feel embarrassed or guilty about getting birth control, out in the open, among adults in a drugstore or clinic. If you want to have sex but feel too embarrassed to get contraception, you need to either reconsider your plans to have intercourse or find a way to cope with your discomfort. You can find a health clinic that has a policy of confidentiality or a drugstore that is not frequented by people you know.

Talking to your partner

Sexual partners need to communicate with each other about birth control in order to make sure they prevent pregnancy. Young people often find it difficult to express their feelings and needs openly with their partners. Pregnancy can easily result from the failure to communicate. For example, a boy may assume that if a girl is willing

Open and honest communication is an essential ingredient to a physical relationship. Teens who find it difficult to talk about birth control with their partner should reconsider whether or not they are ready for sexual intercourse.

to have sex with him, then she is using birth control; in fact, she might not be. Or a girl may feel too shy to insist that a boy use condoms, so she doesn't bring it up and tries just not to think about the risk of pregnancy or sexually transmitted diseases. If you are sexually active, you need to be able to talk openly about birth control with your partner. If you feel you cannot talk about it, think carefully about whether you are ready to have sex with this person.

Young women and men sometimes have sex before they are emotionally ready or prepared with contraception because they fear that turning down sex will make their partner think badly of them. You may feel pressure to have sex in order to make your partner happy, or to try to prove that you are a desirable woman or a real man. You may feel that everyone else is doing it and you will seem uncool if you don't. If you feel this pressure, keep in mind that many teens distort the truth about their sexual exploits; in reality, not everyone is doing it. Furthermore, be assured that your value as a person has nothing to do with when or if you choose to have sex; you deserve to have a partner who appreciates your own value, needs, and feelings. Finally, remember that pregnancy is likely if you have sex without contraception, and remind your partner if you feel any pressure from him or her.

Some young men place the responsibility for birth control on women. Since it is women who become pregnant, men sometimes don't concern themselves about contraception or about the pregnancy that results from unprotected sex. If you think carefully about this attitude, you can easily see its flaws. Men are just as physically

If you have sex

who is responsible for getting the birth control?

involved as women in creating a pregnancy. It is uncaring to make women carry the entire burden. Moreover, if a woman becomes pregnant and keeps the child, the father is legally required to support that child. Contraception should be the concern of both partners.

Talking to parents

Teens considering using birth control are often anxious about their parents' reaction. Young people may even avoid getting birth control out of fear that their parents may find out. It is important to remember that if you have sex without birth control, you will likely get pregnant, and then your parents will have a lot more to be upset about than your use of contraception. You have several choices besides getting pregnant. You can practice abstinence, you may obtain birth control without your parents' knowledge, or talk to your parents about getting contraception.

Talking openly with your parents is usually the best option. It saves you the anxiety of concealing things from them. It also allows them the opportunity to give you useful advice and financial help. It may well be uncomfortable to tell a parent you may plan to have sex, and many parents aren't comfortable hearing it. However, most parents would much rather help their children get contraception than risk pregnancy. They want to protect their children from the difficulties teen pregnancy brings. Often they are grateful to learn that their children are responsible enough to use birth control if they have sex. Parents are usually more understanding than teens give them credit for.

Birth control methods

If you decide to have sexual intercourse, you will need to choose the type of birth control that is most comfortable for you. You can get guidance from parents, other relatives, school counselors or nurses, doctors, or health clinics such as Planned Parenthood. If money is a concern, note that condoms and foam are inexpensive and family planning clinics (found in the Yellow Pages) offer other birth control devices at reduced cost. Whichever method of contraception you choose, be sure to carefully read and follow the instructions that come with the birth control, or else it may not work properly.

Method	How it works	How effective is it?	Side effects	Where to get it	Cost	Protects against STDs?
Condom	Rubber sheath worn on penis; captures sperm so they don't enter vagina.	90–98%. Most effective when used with foam (see below).	None. Rubber around penis may feel awkward.	Drugstore, grocery store. No prescription needed.	Less than 50 cents each.	Yes.
Spermicidal foam	Foam sprayed into vagina before sex; kills sperm.	Not effective alone; when used with condoms, over 99%.	May irritate vagina.	Drugstore, grocery store. No prescription needed.	About $8 for over 20 applications.	Some.
Female condom	Pouch positioned in vagina; keeps sperm from entering reproductive organs.	90–95%	None. May feel awkward.	Drugstore, grocery store. No prescription needed.	About $2.50 each.	Yes.
The pill	Pills taken by woman once every day; contain hormones that prevent ovaries from releasing eggs.	When taken correctly, over 99%.	May include nausea, headaches, depression. Increased risk of high blood pressure, heart problems.	Prescription needed. Doctor, health clinic.	About $30 a month for prescription, plus yearly doctor's fee for checkup.	No.
Diaphragm	Rubber cup filled with spermicide and inserted into vagina before sex; prevents sperm from entering reproductive organs.	94–98%.	Spermicide may irritate vagina. May have greater tendency to bladder infections.	Fitting and prescription needed. Doctor, health clinic.	About $20 for the diaphragm, which lasts around two years, plus doctor's fee for fitting.	Some.
Depovera	Hormone injected into woman's arm; prevents ovaries from releasing eggs.	Over 99%.	May include irregular periods, headaches, nausea, depression.	Doctor, health clinic.	About $40–60 for each injection, which remains effective for 12 weeks.	No.
Norplant	Capsules inserted into woman's arm; contain hormones that prevent ovaries from releasing eggs.	Over 99%.	May include irregular periods, headaches, nausea.	Doctor, health clinic.	$500–700 for an insertion, which lasts for 5 years.	No.

Note that withdrawal, in which the man pulls his penis out of the vagina before he ejaculates, is not a recommended method. Its effectiveness ranges from only 70% to 95%. Even if the man doesn't ejaculate in the vagina, the penis leaks some sperm before ejaculation. If you rely on withdrawal, there is a considerable chance you will get pregnant.

Dealing with an Unplanned Pregnancy

■ Diane was dancing with her boyfriend at the junior prom when he whispered in her ear that he wanted to have sex with her after the dance. She never had sex before, and she didn't really want to, but she also didn't want to disappoint him. She learned about human sexuality and reproduction in her health class, and knew that condoms and other birth control could help prevent pregnancy and diseases. But her boyfriend didn't have a condom, and she thought he would dump her if she said no. Besides, her friends told her that she couldn't get pregnant on her first time.

The following month, Diane couldn't believe that she missed her period. She was shocked and scared, and tried not to think about it. When she didn't get her period again the month after, she knew she had to do something. But what?

When a woman finds out she has unintentionally become pregnant, she is generally stunned. Even if she had sex without birth control and knows that unprotected sex is likely to

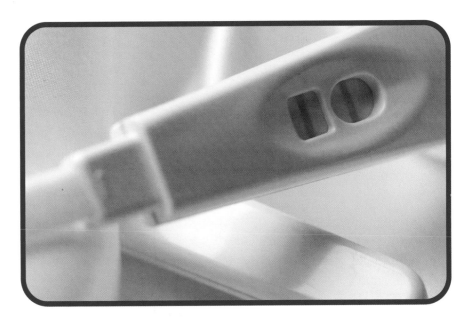

Pregnancy shocks many teens who believe that their age, the infrequency of sexual encounters, or luck will prevent pregnancy. Using birth control is the only way to reduce the risk of an unplanned pregnancy.

result in pregnancy, she may still be shocked. Thinking about the possibility of pregnancy is very different from learning that you are actually pregnant. No matter what a person knows rationally, she may have irrational thoughts like "I'm too young to be pregnant, so this can't be happening," or "I've had sex numerous times and never got pregnant, so I can't be pregnant now." A reaction of shock is especially understandable when the woman did use birth control. Some methods are not as highly reliable as others.

Many teenagers who believe they may be pregnant feel so much disbelief or fear that they try to ignore the possible pregnancy. Often those who are in fact pregnant do not acknowledge the pregnancy for months—sometimes not until they are so big that they can no longer deny it. They often don't tell anyone what is happening, and they sometimes don't even admit the truth to themselves, instead passively hoping that they will figure out what to do sometime in the future. But there are serious problems with this attitude. Pregnant women need to see a doctor to take care of their health and the health of the baby. They also need to make decisions and plans—either to end the pregnancy through abortion, to place the baby for adoption, or to raise the child. The longer women wait to make plans about the pregnancy, the fewer options they will have.

Finding out for sure that you are pregnant and considering your plans as early as possible in the pregnancy gives you the most options, the most control of your future. Getting information, guidance, and emotional support enables you to make the decisions that are wisest for you.

Finding out if you are pregnant

The major early signs of pregnancy are missing a menstrual period or having an unusually light period. If you have sex and the next month do not get your period or have a much shorter period than you usually do, you might be pregnant. You will need to take a test to find out for sure.

If you wish, you can buy a pregnancy test at a drugstore or supermarket and use it in your own bathroom at home. The kit tests your urine to see if contains pregnancy hormones. If the test result is negative, go to a medical professional to double check—sometimes home kits indicate you are not pregnant when in fact you are.

How accurate

is a home pregnancy test?

On the other hand, if the test is positive, then you almost certainly are pregnant—positive results are rarely wrong.

Medical professionals have more accurate pregnancy tests. You can go to a doctor's office, a clinic such as Planned Parenthood, or a hospital. If you are concerned about cost or whether the test will be confidential, ask the staff over the phone and find a place you will be comfortable with. You might also bring a friend or relative for moral support.

Emotions

If you learn you are pregnant, you will likely feel engulfed by emotions. Besides shock, teenagers who find out they are pregnant often feel fear, anger, and dismay. On the other hand, they may also feel excitement, even if they don't wish to have a baby at this time in their lives. Thinking that you are creating a new life may be appealing, as well as scary. It may make you feel suddenly grown up. Pregnant girls and the boys involved usually feel many different emotions all mixed up together. Even more challenging for women, pregnancy releases hormones that intensify emotions.

Pregnant women experience a wide range of emotions because of the hormonal changes that occur during pregnancy. A pregnant teen has the additional challenge of dealing with the anxiety of talking to her parents about an unplanned pregnancy.

It is important to find ways to cope with your emotions. First, remember that many other teenagers have been pregnant and found ways to handle it. If they can manage it, so can you. Second, take care of your health. You need your strength, and getting sick will only make things harder. And third, get information and support from others. Reading books like this one gives you information to work with. Talking with a counselor—at a health clinic, school, or social services agency—can help you sort out your feelings and give you guidance in accordance with your own interests, needs, and circumstances. You can find a counselor by asking the staff who gave you your pregnancy test.

Talking with your parents

Pregnant teenagers often feel fearful of telling others about the pregnancy. However, sharing your feelings with people you trust is important to coping with your emotions and deciding on a course of action. Many pregnant teenagers feel calmer telling their friends or professional counselors than telling their parents. While it is indeed helpful to talk to friends, a counselor, teacher, religious leader—whoever you trust—you also need to consider your parents, however nervous you may feel.

You may imagine that your parents will respond to learning about the pregnancy by being angry with you or disappointed in you. You may worry that your parents will force you to take a course of action you don't want to take. In most cases, however, your fears will not come true. It is understandable that teenagers who have suffered abuse from their parents—physical or emotional harm—choose not to talk with their parents about the pregnancy. Teenagers who are not in an abusive family, however, will nearly always find it helpful to talk with their parents as early in the pregnancy as they can.

How would you tell your mom and dad that you were pregnant?

Generally, parents are upset when they first learn about the pregnancy, just as teenagers are when they first find out. But once the news settles in, most parents are understanding and sympathetic, much more so than teenagers often imagine. The greatest concern of most parents is their children's well-being. They want to help their children—to be an anchor for their children in a storm. Parents have more experience, maturity, and resources than teenagers, and they want to offer emotional and practical support. Discussing your feelings and needs with your parents allows them the opportunity to give you crucial support during what is probably the most serious challenge you have ever faced.

Talking with your partner

It is also recommended that the pregnant woman talk, if possible, with the man involved in creating the pregnancy. First, he will likely want to know about the pregnancy, and second, he may help her sort out a plan of action.

Many teenage men are supportive of their partners. Sometimes, however, problems arise. Some men respond to the news of pregnancy by abandoning the woman. Men should recognize that they are responsible, along with women, for pregnancy. It is only fair, therefore, that the man help the woman with the pregnancy—with caring behavior and, if possible, financial assistance. If the woman gives birth and raises the child, the man is legally required to help her care for the child.

Another problem is that some men try to pressure the woman into making a decision she is not comfortable with. Both partners need to understand that although men are involved with the pregnancy, it is the woman who carries the developing child. Thus, the consequences of decisions about the pregnancy are greatest for the woman. The woman must do what is best for her, even though the man's feelings are important.

What would you do if your boyfriend pressured you to make a decision about an unplanned pregnancy that made you uncomfortable?

When both partners share their feelings openly and listen to each other with sensitivity, they can usually find a way to proceed with the pregnancy that will be comfortable for both of them. If disagreements cannot be resolved, a professional counselor may be helpful. It is good for both partners to share the challenges of pregnancy, but the woman must be careful to focus on her own needs, without being unduly pressured by the man.

Decision making

If you find out you are pregnant, you need to make decisions about how to proceed with the pregnancy. There are three major options: giving birth and raising the child, giving birth and placing the baby for adoption, or ending the pregnancy through abortion. The course of action you choose will carry profound consequences for your health, emotions, finances, and plans for the future. Your decision about how to proceed with your pregnancy is serious and should be made carefully.

Some teenagers feel so overwhelmed by the pregnancy that they avoid thinking about it and simply wish the baby to go away. Obviously, pregnancy will not disappear by simply wishing it. Some teenagers try to force the pregnancy to end by hurting themselves, for example, by purposely falling down stairs. Attempts to force yourself to lose the baby almost always do not work; you will most likely still be pregnant, and the attempt to miscarry will only harm your health and the health of the baby.

Facing the fact that you are pregnant may be difficult, but it need not be overwhelming. Remember that many teenagers become pregnant and handle it very well. Know too that you have the power to decide what to do about your pregnancy. Learning about the three available options enables you to make an informed, rational choice about what is best for you. Discussing your concerns with others also helps you sort out your thoughts and feel supported.

When deciding to raise the child, place the baby for adoption, or have an abortion, you must consider numerous factors in order to determine if it is the best choice for you. How will this option affect you emotionally? Do you have

Pregnant teens should consider their options carefully before making any decisions about an unplanned pregnancy. Parents, teachers, and friends can provide support and guidance for the difficult decisions that must be made, as well as for the emotions that decision creates.

the maturity for this option? The financial resources? How will the option affect your health, your education, your prospects for the future? The remainder of this book will examine the options facing pregnant teenagers.

Being Pregnant

■ Jen and her parents discussed her pregnancy, and they decided together that the best option for her would be to give birth and raise the child with her parents' help. She knew she was lucky to have understanding parents to help her, and she felt so much calmer now that she didn't have to keep her pregnancy a secret.

There were so many things involved with being pregnant that Jen never thought about: trips to the doctor, new eating habits, regular exercise, and saving money for the baby's healthcare. And now she had to be careful with everything she put into her body. Even the medicine she used to take for a headache could harm the baby growing inside her.

Pregnant women who choose the option of adoption, or the option of raising the child themselves, experience the full course of pregnancy. Teenagers are often unprepared for the great changes pregnancy brings to their bodies. It is helpful to know what physical changes to expect. It is especially important to

A pregnancy can be overwhelming, and will influence every aspect of the pregnant woman's life. Every expectant mother, especially teenagers, should seek prenatal care to protect their health and the health of their unborn baby.

understand what a woman needs for her health and the health of the baby. Finally, pregnant women who do not choose abortion need to make plans about the process of giving birth.

Prenatal care

The term **prenatal care** means health care for a pregnant woman and for the embryo developing inside her. Pregnancy is a complex physiological process, and proper care is essential in order to prevent problems. This is especially true for teenagers. Teenagers are more likely than older women to have pregnancy complications, such as **anemia**, **premature birth** of the baby, and giving birth to babies who weigh too little. Studies have shown that a significant reason pregnant teenagers have health problems is that they do not get good prenatal care. On average, one third of American teenagers who give birth did not get sufficient health care during their pregnancies.

An important component of prenatal care is going to a health professional early in the pregnancy and regularly thereafter. Health professionals who treat pregnant women include doctors who specialize in obstetrics/gynecology (called ob/gyns), family practice physicians, and certified nurse-midwives. Nurse-midwives are not doctors but rather are specially licensed to treat women throughout pregnancy and birthing. Some women are more comfortable seeing a nurse-midwife, because the experience often feels less formal than seeing a doctor. Whoever you choose, find someone you feel good about. Ask people you know whom they recommend. If your parents have medical insurance, see if the health practitioner accepts their insurance policy. Low-cost health clinics are also available.

Why should you see a doctor when you are pregnant, even if you feel healthy?

Seeing a health professional is essential during pregnancy. Even if you feel fine, you need to be checked by a doctor or nurse-midwife, because many pregnancy complications are hard to notice yourself. You may have developed high blood pressure or an infection, or the fetus may be lying in an incorrect position—there are a host of risks for a professional to watch out for. Besides treating problems, your health care practitioner will give you special vitamins and guidance on keeping yourself and your baby healthy.

Preventive health care

In addition to seeing a doctor or nurse-midwife regularly, pregnant women also need to take care of their health in their daily lives, in order to prevent complications to themselves and their babies. Good nutrition is critical. While a healthful diet is good for everyone, it is especially important for pregnant women. Pregnant women particularly require protein (found in meats, poultry, fish, cheese, eggs, tofu) and calcium (found in milk, cheese, yogurt, tofu). They also need plenty of fresh fruits and vegetables, which are rich in vitamins and minerals. If you are pregnant, try to cut down on junk food (fast food, chips, sweets). Junk food has a lot of calories but little nutritional value; it will fill you up without giving you the nutrients you could be getting from more wholesome food. Besides eating well, pregnant women also need to drink plenty of fluids—about eight glasses of water or juice each day.

Pregnant teenagers may sometimes find it hard to take care of their physical well-being if they are preoccupied with anxiety about having an unintended pregnancy. Nonetheless, it is important to remember that neglecting your health—eating poorly or missing doctor's visits—can easily result in complications with the pregnancy; then you will have far more to worry about than if you had taken better care of yourself. In addition, healthful living helps reduce feelings of anxiety and stress, enabling you to feel more in control of your emotions.

Regular exercise and adequate sleep are especially important in reducing emotional stress, as well as

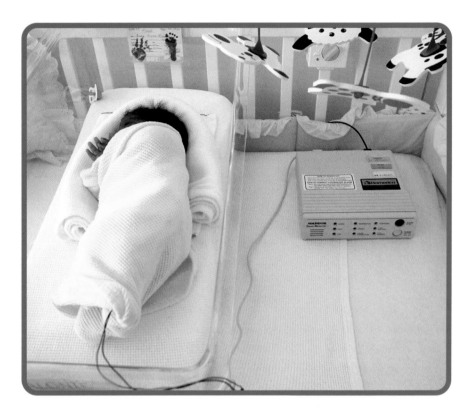

An expectant mother must take good care of herself so that her unborn baby will be healthy. Pregnant women who drink, smoke, or do drugs run the risk of giving birth to a baby who will have lifelong health problems.

promoting physical health. Pregnant women should get plenty of exercise; pregnancy can make you feel tired, but you can find gentle forms of exercise, like walking. Be sure to rest when you need to, and try to get a full night's sleep each night. Your body needs strength.

Finally, pregnant women must avoid cigarettes, recreational drugs, and alcohol, all of which pose major threats to the health of the fetus. Smoking, drinking alcohol, or taking drugs during pregnancy can result in miscarriage (losing the fetus), premature birth of the baby, or serious problems with the baby once he or she is born, including brain damage. If you are pregnant and find it very difficult not to smoke, drink, or use drugs, ask your health practitioner for help.

Is it safe to take

over-the-counter medicine like aspirin if you are pregnant?

Be aware that legal medications, including over-the-counter and prescription medicines, can be as dangerous to a fetus as illegal drugs. Pregnant women must check with their doctor or nurse-midwife about the use of *any* drug, even aspirin. Medications you may have taken without thinking before you got pregnant may be very harmful to use during pregnancy.

Bodily changes during pregnancy

During pregnancy, your body goes through many changes while the fetus develops inside you. Mostly, the changes are normal and natural. For example, in the first 12 weeks of pregnancy, women commonly feel very tired and experience frequent queasiness in the stomach. Pregnancy releases hormones, natural chemicals, that also often have the side effect of making you feel moody and emotional.

As the pregnancy develops between the fourth and ninth month, your abdomen grows larger and you gain weight. You can now feel the fetus moving inside you. Your breasts may feel heavy or occasionally release some fluid. Discomforts in this stage of pregnancy may include indigestion, hemorrhoids, and cramps in the feet and legs. You may also develop backaches from carrying the growing fetus. In the eighth or ninth month, you will likely experience mild contractions in the uterus—this feels like a small tugging or pulling between your hips.

These body changes are typical, but each woman's body is different during pregnancy. A pregnant woman may experience all of these changes or only some of

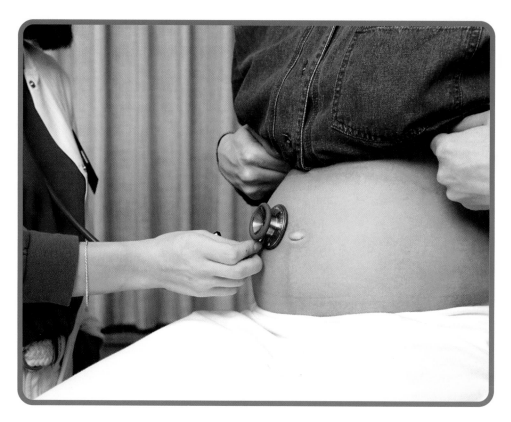

Pregnant women experience many strange sensations not just in their stomachs, but all over their bodies. Hormones released during pregnancy may also make an expectant mother feel moody and emotional.

them. The effects of pregnancy described here may feel strange to you, but they are all normal and usually not too uncomfortable. However, if you are concerned or develop any unusual physical symptoms, be sure to tell your health practitioner.

Delivery

Delivery means birthing the baby, and it begins with what is called **labor**. In labor, you experience intense, frequent contractions in the uterus. The contractions continue until the baby pushes out through the vagina. Most teenagers have normal deliveries. However, if the baby has serious problems coming out, a doctor will need to intervene. In some cases, the doctor needs to pull the baby out by using forceps, a tool that looks like tongs. In other situations, the doctor performs a Cesarian birth: in this procedure, the doctor surgically cuts into the woman's abdomen and removes the baby from her uterus.

Giving birth is physically tough. Early in your pregnancy, you need to discuss labor and delivery with your health practitioner so you can be prepared. You can discuss methods, like breathing techniques, that help you with the pain of labor. You will also need to arrange where to give birth. Most women give birth in the hospital where their health practitioner is affiliated. In some areas, birthing centers are also available; these are facilities that are specially set up for the delivery process and have a more homelike atmosphere than hospitals. Wherever you choose to give birth, arrange in advance to bring someone with you—your parents, a friend, a sibling, whoever you believe will help you feel comfortable.

How would you feel

if you had to give birth without your parents' care and support?

Raising a Child

■ Nicole feels like she hasn't slept much at all in the three months since the birth of her baby boy. He cries a lot during the night, sometimes because he's hungry, sometimes because he needs his diaper changed, and sometimes for no reason at all. Nicole's mom helps out a lot, but she has a job and children of her own. Nicole gets up an hour earlier for school, drops her son off at daycare, goes to class all day, and then comes home straight after school to take care of the baby. She finds it hard to keep up with her schoolwork, and she misses hanging out with her friends. But she knows that her baby is her responsibility, and she does the best that she can.

Close to 50% of American pregnant teenagers give birth and raise their children. Parenting is a serious responsibility. If you do wish to raise a child, consider the decision carefully. Getting accurate information about teen parenthood will help you choose the course of action that is best for you.

A baby depends on its mother for everything – shelter, attention, food, cleaning, and love. Teen mothers must juggle the responsibilities of school, work, and friendships with a newborn baby.

Responsibilities

Most people want to become parents at some point in their lives. However, pregnant teenagers face the prospect of becoming parents at an age when they may not be ready for such a major responsibility. Some pregnant teenagers are attracted to the idea of parenthood—they may fall in love with the magic of a brand new human life. Often a pregnant teenager is excited to imagine having a baby who will love her and need her. On the other hand, teenagers often do not consider the hard responsibilities of raising a child.

Babies are completely dependent on their parents. They need constant care, twenty-four hours a day. They must be fed, diapered, comforted, cared for when they get sick, and watched over at all times to make sure they don't get hurt. This means that parents cannot think of themselves first. They always have to think of the baby. Every day, day in and day out, they must either care for the child themselves or get a trusted babysitter to watch the child temporarily.

Parenting a baby is very demanding, especially for teenagers, who generally don't have the resources and experience with responsibility that adults have. If you are attracted to having a child, be sure you are aware of the hard work involved, as well as the pleasures. It will be years before a child goes to school and gradually develops more independence from you. Parents are responsible for their child for eighteen years.

Money

Raising a child is expensive. Parents must pay for their child's medical expenses, food, clothes, diapers, furniture, bedding, toys, and bottles, among other things. Further, whenever you go to school or work, you must arrange for someone to watch your child—this may be your biggest expense. Your own parents may be able to babysit sometimes, but if they are working or otherwise unavailable, you will need to look for childcare. Private nannies and daycare centers are expensive. Some churches and community centers offer childcare facilities at relatively low cost, but they still cost more money than many teenagers can afford. However, some schools and workplaces provide free childcare. Also, women in low-income families may be eligible to use the state-run Head Start program, which admits preschool children to a learning center each day for free. Check with the program in your state to see if you are eligible.

Many teenagers mistakenly believe that government welfare programs will cover the costs of raising a child. In fact, state programs can be helpful, but they rarely provide enough

Raising a child is expensive; a teen mother must make sure that her baby has medical care, food, shelter, clothing, and daycare. Although government programs will help with some expenses, they do not provide enough assistance to cover everything.

money to make ends meet. Government programs have strict limits on the availability and time span of financial aid. If you, like most teenagers, live with parents who work, you might not be eligible for much government assistance.

Nonetheless, the government does offer some aid to teenage mothers from low-income families. For example, the

Temporary Assistance for Needy Families (TANF) program, commonly called welfare, may provide some money. The Women, Infant, and Children (WIC) program offers low-income mothers coupons for milk, fruit, and other nutritional staples. Government programs are complicated to understand. You can ask a doctor, school nurse or counselor, or community center staff member to help you apply for state assistance.

What would you do

if you and your family could not afford the basic necessities for your newborn baby?

Pregnant teenagers who are considering raising a child must think about the expenses of parenthood and whether or not they have the financial resources to nurture a child for eighteen years. When making a decision, think about how much financial help you can expect from your parents, and about whether the baby's father will help support the child.

The teen parent's family

If you are considering raising a child, you need to talk with your parents about it. Remember that your parents cannot stop you from keeping your baby, nor can they make you raise a child; the choice of childrearing, adoption, or abortion is up to you. But if you choose to rear your child, your decision will affect your parents. Will you move out of the house? Most teen parents continue to live at home. Teenagers usually have too little experience and too little money to live on their own. Thus, their parents have to make adjustments for the new baby.

Your parents must make room in the house for the child and must adapt to the changes in the household that a baby brings—the sound of crying, the pleas for attention, the jumble of toys, the feedings. Moreover, your parents will likely need to help you with the money required to raise a child. Finally, your parents may help you directly with taking care of the child—

The decisions you make don't just affect you, your baby, and the father. Having a baby will also affect your parents' lives, so it is important to have their support when you are raising a child as a teen mother.

with diaper changes, watching and playing with the baby when you are busy, and taking the baby for walks or to the doctor. Most parents are pleased to help care for their grandchildren, and offer invaluable advice and support. Bear in mind, though, that however supportive your parents are, having a new child in the family is an adjustment for them, just as it is for you.

It is helpful to let your parents know that you are aware of the challenges that having a baby brings to the family. Speak with them about what you need from them, and ask them what help they can give you. Knowing before you give birth what to expect from your parents gives you a clearer sense of whether raising a child is the right choice for you. If you do choose to raise the baby, things will go more smoothly if you and your parents have made preparations together.

The baby's father

If you are thinking about raising a child, you also need to consider the role you expect the baby's father to have in the child's upbringing. Talk with him about the decision, if at all possible. As discussed in chapter 2, it is ultimately up to the pregnant woman to decide whether to have the baby or not, but the man is responsible for the pregnancy too. If the woman decides to raise the child, it is best for her and the baby if the man contributes to the baby's care.

Unfortunately, in many cases the man abandons the woman once the child is born, even when he has promised to stick with her. Many pregnant teenage women believe her boyfriend will be there for her and the baby, only to find out otherwise later. If you are considering bearing a child, bear in mind that you cannot know for sure that your boyfriend will help you. If you are considering marriage, keep in mind too that 80% of marriages between teenagers end in divorce.

On the other hand, teen mothers can expect some financial support from the baby's father, given that he has some money available. Even if the man is no longer in contact with the woman, he is required by law to help pay for his child's care. If he does not, the woman can hire a lawyer and ask the court to order him to pay child support. The court will determine how much the man can

How would you feel

if your boyfriend left you when he found out you were pregnant?

afford to pay. Most teenage fathers have little money, but even a little bit helps.

It is harder for both mother and child when the father does not participate in parenting. Besides financial hardship, the mother carries all of the daily work of nurturing the child—work which is rewarding, but also very demanding. While the baby's father is legally required to pay child support monies, it is also good if he can help in the direct care of the child. The child is, after all, his as well as the woman's. He can help feed, bathe, change diapers, and comfort and play with the baby. Many teen fathers want to contribute to raising the child, because they know it is fair to share the responsibility with the woman, because they know it is good for the child, and because there is joy in parenting.

Parenting is a tough responsibility for young men as well as young women. Teen fathers may need to get a job and cut back on spending money on themselves in order to help pay for the child's care. When a man helps raise a child, he has less time for himself, for his friends, for his schoolwork. He must be available for the child's needs.

When thinking about raising a child, both the woman and the man involved in the pregnancy must consider what kind of father the man can be. Will he likely be a reliable father? Does he have the financial resources to contribute to parenting? Is he likely to help the woman with routine child care? If he does not participate in parenting, how well can the woman manage to raise the child without him?

Thinking about your future

Teenagers often don't consider that once you become a parent, you will be a parent for the rest of your life. You will raise the child closely for eighteen years. It is important to look beyond the baby's infancy, toward the future facing you and your child.

Fathers are important to the normal development of children. But, many teen dads don't stick around, even when they promise to. It takes two to make a baby, but most teen mothers raise their children alone.

Your own goals for the future probably include getting an education and a fulfilling career. It is harder to finish high school when you are taking care of a child. Raising a child makes demands on your time, energy, and financial resources. To support your child, you may need to get a job while you are still in high school. Further, it is more difficult to attend college when you have a young child. Will you be able to afford college? Will you have the time to devote to study? You may need to attend classes at night, so that you can work during the day. Who will watch your child? If you cannot go to college, your career opportunities will be limited. Even if you do complete college, it is hard to have the time and energy to get a career going when you must attend to a child's needs.

When considering the future, also be aware that is harder to date, to travel, to meet new people when you are taking care of a child. How will you feel about this in a year, five years, ten? Equally important is your child's future. Do you have the resources to provide a child with the opportunities to flourish? What resources do you expect to have five years from now?

> **Would you be willing**
> to sacrifice your own goals to support and raise your child?

Teen parents usually find in later years that they have set aside wishes of their own in order to take care of their children. Many teen parents are happy with their decision to be parents, but most also feel it would have been better if they had been older when they had children. When adults give birth, they generally have more education, financial resources, and life experience than teenagers, and they may likely be married. Many teenagers who unintentionally become pregnant feel that raising the child is the choice they are most comfortable with; they need to be aware, however, of the consequences.

Teen parenthood is difficult, but it is possible to cope well with its challenges. It is important to find emotional and practical support—from family, friends, school counselors, teachers, as many sources as possible. Government programs and community organizations that offer support to teen parents are also available in many areas. Remember that many teenage parents lead fulfilling lives despite the hardships they face. Raising a child can inspire teenagers to gain maturity, focus, and resourcefulness, in order to meet their responsibilities and attain a bright future for themselves and their children.

Adoption

Megan knows she cannot keep her baby. Her boyfriend abandoned her when he found out she was pregnant, and although her parents were supportive, her family doesn't have enough money to raise another child. But Megan also feels that she can't have an abortion. Both she and her family think having an abortion is wrong.

She discussed her options with her family, and they decided that she should have the baby and place the child for adoption. Megan knew that by doing this, she would give her baby a life with a loving family that will give her child the care and support she is unable to provide.

Pregnant teens who decide they are unable to raise their baby can place their child for adoption. Presently, only 2% to 3% of pregnant teens in the U.S. carry out adoption. Although most pregnant teenagers prefer to become mothers or have an abortion, adoption is an option that some teens feel is best under their circumstances.

Adoption may be the best option for teens who realize they are not ready for a baby, but do not want to have an abortion. Adoption ensures that a baby will have loving parents who can provide support and guidance.

How adoption works

Adoption means that after a woman gives birth, she gives the baby to people who become the child's legal parents. These new parents, called adoptive parents, raise the child as their own. It is important to understand that under the law, adoption is permanent. The woman who gives birth gives up all rights to the child, now and in the future, and is no longer considered the child's parent.

Because adoption is permanent, a pregnant woman considering this choice has to weigh her decision very carefully. Bear in mind, however, that if you choose adoption, it is best to make the arrangements as far in advance as possible before you give birth. This is because the arrangements take time, and you need to ensure that the baby has new parents available right away after birth. If you start adoption procedures after you give birth, the baby will grow older before the adoption is processed. It is harder to find a family for an older child than for a newborn. Moreover, you will find it more painful to let the baby go as more time passes.

Although you should start adoption arrangements before you give birth, under the law you don't sign the final papers that give your baby up until after you give birth. At that time, if you wish, you can spend time thinking and spending time with the baby before making a final decision to give him or her to the adoptive parents. The amount of time varies from state to state, but in all states you are allowed some days or weeks after giving birth in which you can opt out of any adoption procedures.

If you decide

to place your child for adoption, can you change your mind?

Open and closed adoptions

When making adoption arrangements, you will need to decide whether to undertake an open or a closed adoption. In a closed adoption, you give the baby to an agency who places the baby with a new family, but you do not learn who the adoptive parents are. You sign a contract stating that you will seek no contact with the child or the new parents after the adoption takes place. In contrast, an open adoption allows you to be more involved with the new family. You may participate in selecting the adoptive parents, and you may negotiate an agreement with them about keeping in touch with the child.

Where to arrange adoption

There are several ways to arrange adoption. You can go to a government adoption agency, run by the Social Services division of your state, or you can choose a private

Teens who place their babies for adoption often feel hurt and sorrow when their children go to a new family. If you choose adoption, it is important to have strong support system to handle the emotions that follow.

adoption agency that is licensed by the government. (If you choose a private agency, check to make sure it has a state license; if it is not licensed, the adoption is illegal.) The government regulates adoption agencies in order to ensure that they take good care of the birth parents and children. Agencies provide counseling to the birth parents, giving objective advice, support, and guidance. They also go to great lengths to interview and prepare the people who wish to adopt a child, making sure they will be good parents.

Another way to arrange adoption is to hire a private lawyer

who handles adoptions. You can use this method if you have already chosen the people you want to adopt your baby—the people may be, for example, friends of your family. Your lawyer prepares the contracts with the adoptive parents and their lawyer. Note that a lawyer, unlike an agency, does not provide a counselor to help you sort out your personal feelings and decision making. You will need to find knowledgeable adults with whom you can discuss your personal concerns.

Be sure you are comfortable with whomever you choose to arrange the adoption. The lawyer or agency staff should give you a feeling of trust and confidence, and should explain procedures to you in a way you understand. If you don't feel satisfied with one agency or lawyer, you can try another. You can find agencies or lawyers by asking a school counselor, a doctor or health clinic practitioner, or a staff member at the Social Services division of your state government (listed in the Yellow Pages).

Cost

However adoption is arranged, the pregnant woman will have the medical expenses of caring for her pregnancy and delivering the baby. There is ususaly no additional cost to the pregnant woman who organizes adoption through an agency. A private lawyer will charge considerable fees to arrange adoption. Often, adoptive parents agree to pay for all or part of the pregnant woman's medical and legal expenses. If you are concerned about money, consider making such a written agreement. You can state in the agreement that if you change your mind and don't finalize the adoption, you will not have to pay the money back to the adoptive parents.

Talking to your parents and your partner

In the United States, teenage women may legally place their children for adoption without telling their parents.

Under the law, you do not need your parents' permission to place your child for adoption, nor can anyone make you give your child up; the choice is entirely yours, regardless of your age. It is generally best, though, to talk with your parents if you are considering adoption. Your parents can offer you invaluable advice and guidance throughout the decision-making process and the procedure. You and your parents will feel much better if you can communicate your thoughts and feelings and explore them together.

Under the law in most states, the baby's father does have to give permission to place the child for adoption. Check with an adoption agency or lawyer to find out the rules in your state. The baby's father can never force the mother to give the child up for adoption if she does not want to. But if the woman wants to undergo

What would you do

if your baby's father wanted to raise the child, and you wanted to place the baby for adoption?

adoption procedures, the baby's father does usually have the legal right to stop her. If you want to undertake adoption and your partner does not agree, you can seek counseling from a social worker, clergyman or woman, health care clinician, or agency counselor, to try to resolve your differences.

Emotions

Like all the alternatives pregnant teens face, placing a child for adoption is emotionally challenging. Women who choose adoption carry and nourish a fetus inside them for nine months, give birth to the baby, and then give him or her away to another family. It is understandable that they feel sorrow and hurt. On the other hand, they may feel strong and proud that they are giving the child a good home, where he or she can thrive and prosper.

Some women feel guilty about having a child when they

Placing a child in an adoptive family helps the child get the food, clothing, shelter, and love it needs. Sometimes teen mothers want to raise the baby themselves, but realize they cannot provide these things.

are not equipped to be a parent. They may feel that they are letting the child down by turning him or her over to a new family. If you feel this way, remember that although it is indeed unfortunate to have an unwanted pregnancy, that does not make you a bad person. If you feel you cannot raise a child at this time, then you are caring and loving to give the child to people who can. Be assured that the adoptive parents will nurture the child with all of their hearts.

It is difficult to sort out your feelings after placing your child for adoption. Be sure to get emotional support. Talk about your feelings with people you trust—a professional counselor, your parents, relatives, and friends. If you reach out to others and remind yourself that you made the best choice you could under the circumstances, you will likely cope with your emotions and resolve them with time.

Making a choice

Most pregnant teens who don't feel ready to become mothers choose to end the pregnancy through abortion rather than to give birth and place the child for adoption. However, some women are uncomfortable with abortion, or feel it is more positive for them to create a child, or have waited too long in the pregnancy to have an abortion. For a young woman in this circumstance, adoption may be an excellent option.

A woman may decide that adoption is best for the baby, knowing that adoptive parents, besides loving the child as their own, will be well equipped to care for the child. She may wish she could raise the child herself, but knows that she is not old enough to take on the responsibility, that she wants to concentrate on finishing school, or that she would rather wait to have a family until she is grown up with a career, husband, and financial stability. The decision to undergo adoption arrangements may be difficult for her, but she may nonetheless know that it is the right choice for her and the baby.

> **How would you feel**
>
> **if you knew your baby was being adopted by a family that would provide your child with love and support?**

On the other hand, many pregnant teenagers choose not to carry out adoption procedures because they prefer to raise the child themselves. This decision requires a great deal of careful consideration. Many teenagers are not aware of the difficulties involved in parenting.

Abortion

■ Maria had a hard decision to make—she wasn't ready to have a baby while still in high school, and didn't have the support she needed from her family to carry out her pregnancy and place her baby for adoption. She knew she had the option to have an abortion, so she made an appointment at a health clinic to speak with a doctor about what she should expect before, during, and after an abortion.

The doctor told Maria all about the medical procedure—that it was considered safe if it was carried out by a doctor, and that most women didn't experience any long-term physical side effects. The doctor also told her that many women benefited from talking to a counselor to help them deal with their feelings after an abortion. After considering all the information the doctor gave her, Maria decided that having an abortion was her best option.

Abortion means ending a pregnancy by removing the fetus from the woman's body. About 40% (four out of ten) of pregnant teenagers in the United States choose the option of

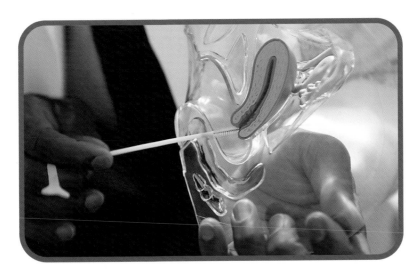

When the fetus is still very small, doctors can use the suction, or aspiration, method of abortion. Confronting the fact that you are pregnant early on gives you the most options. The earlier the decision to have an abortion is made, the easier the medical procedure is on the mother.

abortion. Making the decision to have an abortion can be difficult. Many pregnant teens find that carrying out the pregnancy and assuming the responsibility for the physical, emotional, and financial well-being of their child is more than they can handle. Thus, many teens find that having an abortion is the best alternative for them. Getting accurate information is always helpful in making a decision.

Medical procedure

When performed by a medical professional, abortion is safe and should not interfere with a woman's ability to have a baby in the future.

The most common method is called suction, or aspiration, abortion. This type of abortion must be performed within the first twelve weeks of pregnancy. The procedure is relatively pain-free. It is performed in a doctor's office or clinic—

a hospital is not needed. The doctor inserts a small tube through the woman's vagina into her uterus (the organ which contains the pregnancy). The tube is attached to a suction machine which sucks the embryo (the developing fertilized egg) out of the uterus, thereby ending the pregnancy. The procedure takes about five minutes, and the woman can go home after resting for about an hour.

A similar method of abortion can be performed between 12 and 24 weeks of pregnancy, but the procedure becomes more complicated and expensive the longer the woman has been pregnant. Abortion after 20 weeks is unavailable in some states, and abortion after 24 weeks is prohibited by law throughout the United States. This is why the decision to have an abortion should be made early in the pregnancy. Women who delay making choices about their pregnancies run the risk of finding it is too late to get an abortion.

The need to consider your options early

For example, a young woman may suspect she is pregnant. She's scared, so she tries to just not think about it. She doesn't want to know she's pregnant, and she doesn't want her parents to find out. By the time her pregnancy is so advanced that she can no longer deny it, she goes to a clinic and learns that she is over 20 weeks pregnant—past the time limit for abortions in her state. Now she has lost the choice to end her pregnancy. She and her family will have to cope with having the baby, whether they would have chosen to or not.

Emotions

Some women experience feelings of sadness and anger about having had an unwanted pregnancy and about ending it. These feelings are normal and usually diminish with time. However, if they are troublesome, counseling is recommended. Feelings of relief after an abortion are also common. Often different feelings are mixed together. If you or your girl-friend have had an abortion, it is important that you turn to others to help you cope with your feelings and sort them out. Talk to your parents, relatives, friends, or doctor—whoever you trust to be there for you. It is also helpful to remember that even if you have painful feelings about the abortion, you made what you believe was the best choice possible for you under the circumstances of teen pregnancy.

Cost

Abortion, like all medical procedures, can be expensive. Some teens have difficulty finding ways to pay for an abortion in time to obtain the suction procedure. All options facing pregnant teens carry financial burdens.

Emotions run high during pregnancy and can become complicated at the prospect of an abortion. Establishing a support network with family, friends, and your partner can help you sort out these feelings and decide if you are making the right decision.

How would you feel

to no longer be pregnant after you had an abortion?

Federal Medicaid does not pay for abortion, but some states do provide funding for low-income women to have the procedure. In addition, some clinics provide abortions at low cost. Family doctors, school nurses, medical clinics, and Planned Parenthood are good sources for information on this matter. The girl's expense can also be reduced if the male involved in the pregnancy helps pay for the procedure. The girl and boy should definitely discuss his financial contribution, if at all possible. Finally, the pregnant girl's parents may provide financial help. If they have health insurance, it may cover the cost of their daughter's abortion.

Legality

Abortion is legal in the United States. Some Americans oppose this, but polls consistently show that the majority agree with the law that every woman has the right to choose whether or not to have an abortion. Federal law prohibits abortion only after 24 weeks of pregnancy (as mentioned earlier, some states prohibit abortions after 20 weeks).

Some states have special laws that apply to teenagers seeking abortions. These laws, called parental notification laws, state that women under 18 must have their parents' permission to have an abortion. A doctor, clinic, or school counselor or nurse can tell you if your state has such a law. Some states with these laws require only one parent to give permission, while other states require both parents to consent to their daughter's abortion. Laws requiring the permission of both parents may cause difficulty to teenagers whose parents are divorced and who may not have contact with one of their parents. Regardless of the specifics, a teenager who feels unable to meet the requirements of their state's parental notification law may go before a judge and seek an exemption from the law. Some clinics, including Planned Parenthood, offer teenagers assistance with this court procedure.

How would you tell

your parents that you wanted to have an abortion?

Talking to parents

Most teenagers who consider having an abortion do talk with their parents about it, whether or not they are required to do so by law. It is understandable that those girls who suffer physical or emotional abuse by their parents, or whose pregnancy was caused by a parent's sexual abuse, may not feel able to tell their parents that they are pregnant and want to have an abortion. Girls in this circumstance should find other adults, such as counselors, who they can turn to with trust that what they discuss will be confidential. In all other cases, it is best to talk with your parents.

Talking with your parents or another adult, like a doctor, can help you make the right decision about abortion. Adults can offer experience, guidance, and emotional and financial support.

As discussed in Chapter 2, as adults, parents can offer invaluable knowledge and experience to teenagers confronting tough issues for the first time. Most parents place the highest value on their children's welfare and are therefore in the ideal position to help you determine whether or not an abortion is the best choice for you. If you do elect to have an abortion, they can help you to find a good doctor or clinic, as well as provide financial assistance. Perhaps even more importantly, parents can be your best source of emotional support.

Some teens believe that their parents will try to make the decision about abortion for them. Some parents may have strong religious beliefs against abortion. However, if you tell your parents how you feel, in most cases you will discover that your parents will be understanding and flexible; they want to help you do what is in your own best interest. That is why it is important to talk to your parents, even if you are frightened to.

You will probably be surprised once you open up to them, sparing yourself needless anxiety and allowing your parents to provide the support they would like to offer. On the other hand, if you do meet opposition from your parents, it can be very confusing and stressful for the entire family. Most disagreements can be worked out over time, but abortion has a relatively brief time limit. It is best in this case to seek professional counseling to help you decide what you want to do about your pregnancy and to learn how to cope with family tension.

Talking to others

Most medical facilities that offer abortions also provide counseling. Parental notification laws do not cover counseling, so all teens are legally entitled to receive counseling from abortion providers, with or without their parents' knowledge. Counseling is useful in making a decision about abortion, and it is especially important when a teen does elect abortion. The trained professional can answer questions, provide information

Would you want

to talk to a counselor after you had an abortion?

about the procedure, and help the young woman sort out her feelings.

Finally, a teen considering abortion should discuss it with the male who impregnated her, unless she has strong, sound reasons not to. He will probably want to be involved in the decision making process, but he must be aware that the choice to have an abortion or not is ultimately the girl's to make, not his, as it is her body that is under consideration. This can be hard for some boys to accept, and he may wish to see a counselor to help him work through his concerns. It is good for him to voice his feelings to his partner and for her to listen to them, but he must respect her final choice. Conversely, she must make her own decision about abortion, without letting a boyfriend pressure or unduly influence her. He has no legal authority to do so.

Making a choice

Under U.S. law, no one, including your parents, can make you have an abortion against your will. Each woman can determine for herself whether she wants an abortion or not. In making the decision, she must consider the alternatives—raising a child or placing the child in an adoptive home.

Talk to your partner. Each parent has legal rights and responsibilities. Shutting out a partner who wants to be involved will only create negative feelings that complicate the situation.

The major reason pregnant teenagers choose abortion is they feel unable or unwilling to undergo the alternatives. Some common reasons teenagers don't elect to have an abortion are: they have strong religious beliefs against abortion; they postpone making any decisions until the opportunity for abortion is past; they don't know where to go to obtain an abortion; they don't realize the full responsibility involved in having a baby. In all cases, getting accurate information and discussing it with objective people gives teens the power they need to make an informed choice. Whatever a girl chooses to do, it is important that she consider all of her options, so that she can be sure that she takes the best course of action for herself.

To learn more about teen pregnancy and the options of raising the child, placing the baby for adoption, and having an abortion, see the resources listed at the end of this book. Seek out other teenagers you may know who have been pregnant or are raising children. Be sure also to talk with adults whom you trust will give you the help you need.

Glossary

Abortion – ending a pregnancy through a medical procedure that removes the embryo from the uterus.

Abstinence – refraining from sexual activity.

Adoption – a permanent arrangement in which a mother gives her child to someone who becomes the child's legal parents.

Anemia – a condition in which the blood is deficient in red blood cells or iron.

Birth control – devices or methods that block the fertilization of the egg by the sperm to prevent pregnancy.

Contraception – birth control.

Delivery – the process of giving birth to a baby.

Labor – a period of intense, frequent contractions of the uterus that precedes birth.

Premature birth – a birth that occurs before 37 weeks of pregnancy.

Prenatal care – medical care for the pregnant woman and the fetus developing inside her.

Sexual intercourse – insertion of the penis into the vagina.

Sexually transmitted disease (STD) – a disease, like the HIV virus that causes AIDS, that is transmitted from one person to another during sexual intercourse.

Further Reading

Books

Arthur, Shirley. *Surviving Teen Pregnancy: Your Choices, Dreams, and Decisions*. Revised ed. Buena Park, CA: Morning Glory Press, 1996.

Bell, Ruth. *Changing Bodies, Changing Lives*. Revised ed. New York: Random House, 1987.

Bode, Janet. *Kids Still Having Kids: Talking About Teen Pregnancy*. Danbury, CT: Franklin Watts, 1999.

Jamiolkowski, Raymond. *A Baby Doesn't Make the Man: Alternative Sources of Power and Manhood for Young Men*. New York: Rosen Publishing Group, 1997.

Websites

www.plannedparenthood.com

www.teenwire.com

www.teenpregnancy.org

www.birthmother.com

www.cfoc.org

Index

Abortion, 9, 20, 24, 38,
  52-59
  costs of, 55-56, 57
  counselors for, 57, 58
  decision on, 59
  definition of, 52
  early planning for, 54
  and emotions, 54-55
  and legal issues, 54, 56
  and male partner, 55-56,
    58-59
  and parents, 56-58
  and popularity of
    decision, 44, 51, 52-53
  procedure for, 53-54
  timing for, 53, 54, 55,
    56, 58
Abstinence, 11-12
Adoption, 9, 20, 24, 26,
  38, 44-51
  with agencies for, 46-47,
    48, 49
  arrangements for,
    46-48
  counselors for, 48, 49
  decision on, 51
  and emotions, 49-51
  lawyer for, 47-48, 49
  and male partner, 49
  open and closed, 46
  and parents, 48-49
  and popularity of
    decision, 44
  process of, 45-46
Anemia, 28
Birth control, 9, 10
  communication between
    partners on, 13-15
  cost of, 12, 16

counselors for, 16
and culture, 12, 13
information on, 12, 16-17
low-cost, 12, 16
methods of, 11-12, 16-17,
  19
planning for, 12
pregnancy prevented
  with, 9-10, 11, 14
reason for teens not
  using, 12-13
responsibility for, 15
and substance abuse, 13
Birthing centers, 33
Cesarian birth, 33
Condoms, 17, 19
Contraception. *See* Birth
  control
Contractions, 31, 32-33
Daycare centers, 36
Delivery, 28, 32-33
Depovera, 17
Diaphragm, 17
Doctor
  and abortion, 55
  and adoption, 48
  and birth control, 16
  and delivery, 33
  and pregnancy tests, 20
  and prenatal care, 28-29,
    31, 32
  and state assistance, 38
Female condom, 17
Forceps, 33
Government
  and adoption, 46, 47, 48
  and aid to teen mothers,
    36-38, 43
Head Start, 36

Health clinics, 16, 20, 28,
  55, 56
Hormones, 21, 31
Labor, 32-33
Male partner/father
  abandonment by, 40
  and abortion, 55-56,
    58-59
  and adoption, 49
  and birth control, 15-16
  and child support, 15,
    23, 24, 38, 40-41
  and emotions on
    pregnancy, 21
  pregnant woman talking
    with, 23-24
  and pressure to have
    intercourse, 15
  and raising child, 40-41
Marriage, and divorce, 40
Menstrual period, 20
Miscarriage, 24, 30
  See also Abortion
Nannies, 36
Norplant, 17
Nurse-midwives, 28-29,
  31
Parental notification laws,
  56, 58
Pill, 17
Planned Parenthood, 16,
  20, 55, 56
Pregnancy, 26-33
  biology of, 10-11
  and bodily changes,
    31-33
  complications of, 28-29,
    30-31
  counselors for, 21-22

Index

and delivery, 28, 32-33
and diet, 29
and emotions, 21-22, 29
and exercise, 29-30
information about, 9
and legal drugs, 31
and prenatal care, 20,
  27-29
and preventive health
  care, 20, 21, 29-31
signs of, 20
and sleep, 29-30
and smoking, 30
and substance abuse,
  30-31
Pregnancy tests, 20-21
Premature birth, 28, 30
Prenatal care, 20, 27-29
Raising child, 9, 16, 20,
  24, 26, 34-43, 51
  and baby's father, 40-41
  and babysitters, 36
  and career, 42-43, 51
  and child support, 15,
    23, 24, 38, 40-41

and education, 42-43, 51
for eighteen years, 36, 41
and future, 41-43
and parents, 36, 37,
  38-40
and popularity of
  decision, 34
responsibilities of, 35-36
and socializing, 43
Sexual intercourse, 9,
  10-11
and culture, 12, 13
decision to have, 11-12
and emotional readiness,
  11, 15
pressure to have, 15
without birth control,
  10-11, 12, 15
Sexually transmitted
  diseases, 11, 12, 15
Social Services, and
  adoption, 46, 48
Spermicidal foam, 17, 19
Suction (aspiration)
  abortion, 53-54, 55

Temporary Assistance
  for Needy Families
  program, 38
Unplanned pregnancies,
  18-25
  and counselor, 21-22, 23
  decisions on, 20, 23,
    24-25, 38, 40-41.
    See also Abortion;
    Adoption; Raising
    child
  denial of, 19-20, 24
  and emotions, 18-19,
    21-22, 29
  and male partner, 23-24
  and miscarriage
    attempts, 24
  number of, 8, 12
  and parents, 22-23
Uterus, 31, 32, 54
Withdrawal, 17
Women, Infant, and
  Children program, 38

About the Author

Michele Alpern is the author of numerous works on social issues, including *The Effects of Job Loss on the Family* (Chelsea House, 2002), and has also written books on Iraq and Turkey. She is a Ph.D. candidate at Rutgers University. She is also an artist.

About the Editor

Marvin Rosen is a licensed clinical psychologist who practices in Media, Pennsylvania. He received his doctorate degree from the University of Pennsylvania in 1961. Since 1963, he has worked with intellectually and emotionally challenged people at Elwyn, Inc. in Pennsylvania, with clinical, administrative, research, and training responsibilities. He also conducts a private practice of psychology. Dr. Rosen has taught psychology at the University of Pennsylvania, Bryn Mawr College, and West Chester University. He has written or edited seven book and numerous professional articles in the areas of psychology, rehabilitation, emotional disturbance, and mental retardation.